*blackbirds don't mate with starlings*

Janaka Malwatta was born in Kandy, the hill capital of Sri Lanka, grew up in London, and moved to Brisbane in 2010. He writes poems about his experiences as an immigrant in two continents. He also writes narrative poetry, often exploring Sri Lankan stories. He has performed poetry in Brisbane, including at the Queensland Poetry Festival, and has been published in *Cordite Poetry Review*, *Rabbit Poetry* and *Peril* magazine. He was the Sri Lankan voice on the ESPNCricinfo.com blog *The Cordon*. He is one half of the poetry and tabla collective Dubla. *blackbirds don't mate with starlings* is his first full-length poetry collection.

# Janaka **Malwatta**

blackbirds don't mate
with starlings

First published 2022 by University of Queensland Press
PO Box 6042, St Lucia, Queensland 4067 Australia

University of Queensland Press (UQP) acknowledges the Traditional Owners and
their custodianship of the lands on which UQP operates. We pay our respects to their
Ancestors and their descendants, who continue cultural and spiritual connections to
Country. We recognise their valuable contributions to Australian and global society.

uqp.com.au
reception@uqp.com.au

Cover design by Sandy Cull
Author photograph by Nandhaka Pieris
Typeset in 11.5/14 pt Adobe Garamond Pro by Post Pre-press Group, Brisbane
Printed in Australia by McPherson's Printing Group

 **Queensland Government** University of Queensland Press is supported by the Queensland
Government through Arts Queensland.

   University of Queensland Press is assisted by
the Australian Government through the
Australia Council, its arts funding and advisory
body.

A catalogue record for this book is available from the National Library of Australia.

ISBN 978 0 7022 6572 3 (pbk)
ISBN 978 0 7022 6715 4 (epdf)

University of Queensland Press uses papers that are natural, renewable and recyclable
products made from wood grown in well-managed forests and other controlled sources.
The logging and manufacturing processes conform to the environmental regulations of
the country of origin.

*dedicated to*

තාත්ති

# Contents

**foundlings**

unburdenings

## phrases from my youth

does that colour wash off
is your willy brown as well
do you always eat curry


nig-nog
wog
coon


you weren't born here
you don't belong here


paki
go home paki
paki go home


i was born here
my father was born here
my grandfather was born here –
that's what counts


ain't no black
in the union jack

black and white
unite and fight
pakis must go home


i don't like pakis
i don't mind blacks
but i don't like pakis
i don't know why


can i call you jonathan

# I am/am I

Sinhalese
Sri Lankan
Asian

Brisbanite
Queenslander
Australian

Londoner
British
European

# swastika

some coward carved a swastika on my door
if I'd seen him I'd have asked him
you trying to make me feel at home
we have thousands of these back there
inset in lintels
in stone steps in our temples
but they're usually gold, brother
you need to raise your game

Buddhists Hindus Jains
have revered this symbol for centuries
when you say swastika you're speaking Sanskrit
an Asian tongue in your mouth
Asian art you're inscribing on my door

this was our symbol before it was yours
you can't have it for your hate it's not yours to take
and besides those lines are all over the place
that cross ain't straight that angle ain't right
those arms you've carved are different heights
as a piece of craftmanship

it's a disgrace
if that's the best you can do
no wonder all you have
is hate

# triptych – past present future

I'm middle-aged overweight tyres around my waist
when I see them pull down statues their rage is my rage
their anger is my anger it comes from the same place
I've got a lifetime of it built up you're with me or in my way

skinny little brown boy immigrant fresh
they're quick to show you you're different from the rest
went from sunny skies of home where brown was all I'd known
to grey clouds and cold where brown meant you stood alone

racist kids weren't the problem it was racist teachers
who used their power to put you down and the history they teach us
those distorted stories is where this cancer starts
you're going to have a warped view if you don't know your past

they sanitise their stories
emphasise their glories
don't tell you how deep the gore is
or how twisted the lore is
don't let your schooling get in the way of your education son

they tell you Wilberforce freed the slaves
don't tell you Haiti freed itself
then slave-owning nations made it pay reparations
21 billion till 1947
now you understand why it's an impoverished nation

Britain paid compensation when it set the slaves free
paid to those who held slaves in captivity
300 billion in today's currency
from 1835 to 2015
that debt to slave-owning families
was paid no matter the colour of your skin
by every British taxpayer there's ever been
including me

Namdharis and sepoys tied to cannons backs arched
heads flew forty feet when they detonated the charge

Churchill's Bengal famine killed more than three million
you could interchange photos from Bengal and Belsen
the difference you'll see is the colour of the victims

while Conran and Quant made their names
on the King's Road
in the queen's name
the British built concentration camps
hooked men to wires ramped up the amps
broken bottles in vaginas sliced off testes
beat Kikuyu to death while starvation and disease
took their families

these are the savages who say they civilised us
built our schools built our railways built our countries from the dust
for all this they say we should give them thanks
did they forget to tell you they made their money off our backs

this is empire's story and we're all empire's children
they're fooling you and me with these tales they're telling
it's called 'whitewashed' for a reason they left the truth on the shelf
they don't have the courage to be honest with themselves

*present*

they tell me it's old news belongs in the past
but the past casts long shadows
old hatreds still flow
through our streets and offices
trickle down to police officers
we've all got stories we've all got scars

George's cousin on ICU
they took a two-by-four broke his jaw in two
since they jumped on him Hanif's hand is a claw
can't pick up a cup hold a pen any more
old news old news belongs in the past

ten skinheads caught Chandran by his doorstep
used his body for a dance floor a bovver boot quickstep
got a tube down his throat hooked up to machines
a patient in the hospital he was studying in
old news old news

if you escape the violence other hurdles await
you're in the same team but you're playing a different game
Dave said it doesn't matter if you're better than them
you have to work twice as hard to be level with them
forty years ago my mother told me the same
it's still true now it was true back then
the things we've done to keep those dreams alive
let me tell you some stories of how we survived

with the change of a letter Shah became Shaw
all those jobs he'd applied for which had passed him by before

suddenly he's got one got his new name on the door
when he looks in the mirror I wonder what he sees
the man he was or the man he's had to be
does he ever wonder is this my legacy
children you can't be yourselves and compete
this is an old song we're just singing the chorus
our Jewish brothers sang this song before us
tell me why
to find
the level playing field
I have to erase what it means
to be me

his boss called him darkie threw scalpels at him
he had to stand there take it on the chin
if he'd said anything then
it would have come back to him
he's a boss now surgeon best in the game
Savile Row suited Joseph Cheaney booted
but those pinstripes are prison bars
they constrain the pain
not from the scalpel's point but from the shame
of enduring in silence
when your thoughts are full of violence
if you let them get away with it
it always leaves a stain

*future*

this is for those who came before
who endured far more than we endure
and the young generation next in line
this story will become your story in time

that means you my son
you are now the same age I was
when I sat on that stool first day in school
new country new city new classroom
rest of the kids cross-legged on the floor
stuck out like a sore thumb from day one
never got any better from there on

blue jumper with red-and-white trim
don't know whether my folks thought
the union jack colours would help me fit in
or whether it was all we had immigrant fresh
they didn't know they were dropping me
in the vipers' nest
but I know what lies ahead for you
I can't protect you from this you know I would if I could
take all the body blows I've had a lifetime of those
a few more will make no difference to me now

you will have to grow strong
let's not pretend
you will run the same race as your white friends
but remember no-one can change you

only you can do that
your self-esteem is in your own hands
know yourself know your history
be proud of who you are

Ungi your grandmother's mother
was four foot and not much but she stood up
for what she believed
headmistress of a Buddhist school when the British
were trying to wipe us out in our own country
can you imagine the battles she fought

Aaththa your father's grandmother taught
Abhidhamma to priests
published her first book in her eighties
criss-crossed the country with her charities
these people never stopped

Wai Por your mother's mother left school at fourteen
because educating daughters was a waste of time
carried a load on her shoulders up every day before five
she made sure her daughters got their degrees

Aachchi your father's mother became
a consultant surgeon when female surgeons were
rare and Asian surgeons were rare
and female Asian surgeons didn't exist
except in the imaginations of those few women
who pushed back the boundaries of the old boys'
brigade and didn't give in

did you notice
the women in our family have been fighters
we all have it in us you do too
I haven't even told you what your grandfathers used to do
if you have to choose between fitting in and being you
you need to know the right thing is not the easy thing
but it's easier than caving in
that's short-term gain for long-term pain
don't play their game
look them in the eye say it with me
you'll never change what it means to be me

examinings

# blackbirds and starlings

*(conversation nurses' station Barnet General Hospital 1994)*

What you doing with him?
Couldn't you get a proper bloke?
A white bloke?
I seen you with him up the High Street
holding hands and that
It's not right
You want to stick to your own kind
He'll let you down, you know
his sort always do
Probably married to a cousin or something
Here, where you going?
What you got the hump for?
I'm only telling you for your own good
Blackbirds don't mate with starlings

## conversation doctor's consulting room
## Brisbane 2013

They tell me I'll never work again
not with my arm like this.
Look at it. Can't even hold a cup of tea.
Can you see me up on the scaffolding?
Centrelink knocked me back.
They don't care.
A hundred and fifty dollars a fortnight.
That's all they gave me.
Could you live on that?
They weren't interested in anything the hospital said.
All those doctors. All those reports.
Just knocked me back.
Spotty little kid
looks like a fucking teenager
stares at a computer screen
won't even look you in the eye
click click click and that's it.
A hundred and fifty dollars.
And you know what shits me?
Please don't be offended
but they give those
black
cunts
everything.
For nothing.
Just 'cos they're black.
Debbie works in a care home.

There's a woman there, she gets
six hundred dollars and another six hundred
just 'cos she's an islander.
Torres Strait. Something. I don't know.
Can you believe that?
And there's me. Worked all my life
every day since I came to this country.
What do I get?
Two hundred dollars. And 'cos I got savings
they take fifty dollars off you.
They punish you for working all your life.
But these black cunts ...
they just sit around and get
everything given to them.
I don't mean you.
You're working. You pay taxes.
I worked my whole life.
Can't lift a fucking cup of tea
and I get nothing.
Black cunts.

## conversation barbeque Brisbane inner west 2012

when I worked in the mines
            *chortles*
this young Islander turned up one day
            *sweeps hand through wisps of white hair*
huge long name
            *quick swig of Sauv Blanc*
far too difficult for us
            *cheeks redden in uneven blotches*
so we said to him
            *crow's feet wrinkle as he grins*
what day is it today? Sunday?
            *shoulder-shaking chuckle*
that's what we'll call you
            *guffaw*
we called him Sunday the whole time he was there
            *jowls wobble with mirth*

# how dare they

how dare they pull down that statue
how dare they deface war memorials
how dare they call Churchill (the racist) a racist
why don't they play by the rules

the rules which have never been applied to them

the rules which didn't apply to
Cherry Groce mother of six
paralysed when police
shot her in her
own bed

Cynthia Jarrett grandmother
they arrested her son illegal stop
and search searched her home too
then she arrested cardiac
arrest heart stopped
for good

Christopher Alder war veteran
died in a police cell face
down handcuffed trousers pulled
down four officers over him
making monkey noises

countless others

if the rules don't apply to them
why should they apply the rules

**you say**


you say of course black lives matter all lives matter
you say there is no such thing as white privilege
you say white fragility is a racist concept
you say they are trying to rewrite history
you say of course we are friends we have
known each other for twenty years

I say
have we

# passfail

*(poem written in response to a question posed by* Peril *magazine: what does it mean exactly to be 'Australian' – what does it take to pass? what does it take to fail?)*

Speak with an Aussie or English accent: pass
Amusingly mispronounce words in a Spanish
lilt or with a Gallic shrug: bare pass
Mispronounce words with a broad
Indian drawl or scissor-sharp Chinese vowels: fail

Use an Anglo name: pass
Smile when asked, 'I can't say your name.
Can I call you John?': bare pass
Reply, 'Sure. Can I call you fuckwit?': fail

Never speak your language outside your home: pass
If you do, nod sheepishly when told,
'This is Australia; speak English': fail
Reply to the same question with,
'I don't see you speaking Turrbal': clear fail

Wear a cross: pass
Wear a rakhi: it will be assumed
you have just been to a festival – pass
Wear a turban or a hijab: you're obviously
not even trying

imaginings

# LONDON

## desert rat, part 1

Adil has sand-coloured skin.
The grit and bite of the desert lie on him
handed down, with his pinched face,
from North African forefathers he can no longer trace.
He's five foot four, five-five if he stretches
and eight stone wringing wet.
*I seen more fat on a crisp* they'd say
when he first arrived and he'd always smile
not understanding a word they said.

His mother has eyes rimmed with kohl and despair.
This is not the life she chose.
They were blown to this country by fierce desert winds
carried by calamity and kindling hope.
They're strangers in a cold land
with nowhere else to go.

They thought they traded warmth for safety
found themselves in South London's high-rises
tower blocks erupting from the streets
like concrete exclamation marks
wind-blown, but not by warm desert winds
there's no sirocco here: wind tunnels
wind funnelled between concrete blocks
grey clouds, cold rain and fear.

This is a no-go area for cops.
If they come at all, they come in vans.
Wire cages wrap round the shops.
You don't come here unless you belong.

Where Adil grows up, people hide
behind doors locked behind iron grilles.
You don't walk down dark corridors
even in daylight
and stairwells are all pools of piss.
Desert Rat, they call him here, and worse
children of immigrants spewing the same curse
soaked in the bile of centuries
that their parents received when they arrived.
This is not a place to make friends.
This is a place to survive.

Adil needs an edge and it comes in the shape
of six inches of steel narrowed to a point
with a weight of hate behind it.
He doesn't leave home without it.
By the time he leaves school he's learnt
life is a two-room flat behind an iron grille
if he wants anything, he has to take it
and the distance between him and the people around him
is as vast as the distance between him and his homeland.
This place is run by rules he can't understand
except one: his knife talks better than he can.

In a voice dripping with honeyed apricots
his mother tells him stories of his desert home.
He half-remembers a land of warmth
flatbreads on the fire at family gatherings
being passed hand to hand
mother to aunt to cousin to aunt
a Pass the Parcel smothered in layers
of love waiting to be unwrapped.
And afterwards, the greatest warmth of all:
maternal flesh enveloping him as he slept.

Other memories too, he carries
memories his mother won't discuss.
A man, tight curly brown hair.
He has Adil's pinched face
or maybe Adil has his.
She called him 'her dreamer' when they first met
head full of ideas, ideas that didn't fit.
Who would have thought that gentle man
with his shy smile would have the strength
to be so defiant?

Adil can still hear his mother's screams
when they took him away for the last time.
Sometimes he hears her in his dreams
sometimes in the room next door.
A series of scars works its way up his arm
a ladder of pain which runs straight from
the point of the blade he always carries
to the well of sorrow inside him

letting the pain out
the only way he knows.
And, deeper still
the secret he can't share.
For all this, he blames the man
with the tight curly hair.

Adil's sharp eyed and light fingered
thin enough to squeeze through gaps
most don't even see.
And if it comes to it, fast, boy, he can run.
It's a living, of sorts.
He sees an old man and an open door.
The old man asks him a question he ignores.
As Adil brushes past, he hears the man whisper
*Is it 1944?*
Adil's forgotten the old man's there
as he rifles through cupboards and drawers.
Behind him, the old man watches benignly
like an indulgent grandfather
until Adil reaches for the fistful of medals
in the last drawer he opens.

Adil is surprised by a grip on his wrist.
He turns 'round to see a checked shirt, crumpled
and foodstained, and a blueveined hand
grasping him, shaking but still holding tightly
stronger than he expected.

The old man is standing between him and the door.

# desert rat, part 2

Billy has lived with Betty for a lifetime.
Old now, she has wounds on her legs
craters running deep from skin to bone.
They've moved from pills and potions
to a cure handed down the centuries.
Maggots crawl over her legs eating
live bacteria and dead flesh
because sometimes you have to
go backwards to go forwards
even if it is eight hundred years.
In countries where piped water is a pipe dream
they use the surgeon's knife to cut away dead skin
knowing they've reached healthy tissue
when the patient screams;
maybe the maggots aren't so bad.

Billy cares for her in their home
where the wallpaper hasn't changed
in fifty years.
Every mantelpiece, table, shelf
is crowded with clusters of framed
photos in which children, grandchildren,
their grandchildren's children
gurn and gurgle behind glass.
Pushed to a corner hidden
behind gap-toothed grins
and wedding day smiles
is a faded black and white.

A man in an army uniform
pressed and clean;
a woman in a cotton dress
with eyes that gleam.

You see, when Billy was born
cars were horse-drawn.
Gaslights lit up the evening sky.
The fields of Europe were ploughed
by shells. Men died in trenches without
knowing why. When Chaplin made his first
film Billy was ten. He was a grandfather
when Armstrong walked on the moon
and long retired when the Berlin Wall fell.

Billy moved to their house when it was first built.
He left only to go to war in Europe
and found himself in a desert instead.
When it was his turn to fight for King and Country
there had been progress:
no longer content with bombing their own cities
pink-faced Europeans scorched a
trail of destruction across desert sands
fighting a European war
under African skies.
Desert Rats, they called them
following Monty on the trail of a Fox
squatting for months in a metal box
hotter than an oven.

He'd courted Betty, the girl next door
in the years between the wars
when courting meant home by nine and
no funny business.
Despite the ulcers and wandering mind
and skin which tears like paper
Billy can still see the woman in the cotton dress
with the eyes that gleam.
Every morning he makes her tea
two sugars and full fat milk
no matter what the doctors say
and helps her brush her hair.
He's happy, he says, because
love isn't all about dancing and funny business.

When the nurses come to tend to her legs
Billy's always immaculately dressed
tie knotted, clean-shaven, trousers pressed
he's smarter than them, that's for sure.
Every now and again, he has a bit of fun.
*I remember when all this was fields* he says.
The nurses look at each other, eyes rolling.
*The old man's off again* they're thinking.
He can see it in their faces

                              but the joke's on them.
Billy knows his house was built on a farm.
The street names – Meadow Road, Home Coppice
– are not some planner's fancy.

He remembers, outside his front door
a huge oak, weatherworn but strong.
The local kids used to climb it
dangle on a swing someone's father
had nailed to its boughs.
It was their Xbox, Nintendo and PS2.
Underneath his feet they buried its roots
covering it in the concrete of a South London estate.

After Betty's death, Billy finds it harder
to get up in the mornings, iron his shirt.
There's no-one to make tea for
no hair to brush and no visiting nurses
to break up the day.
He hates himself for thinking it
but Betty's illness was his social life.

He's more forgetful
puts his electric kettle on the gas hob
and wanders out of the house
all hours of the day.
By the time he's walked down the front path
he's forgotten why he left.
One day, leaning on his gate, not quite sure
how he's got there, he asks
*Is it 1944?*
of a passing boy
with a pinched face
and sand-coloured skin.

The boy brushes past Billy, goes through the open door.
Billy stares after him for a while, then shuffles back inside.
He watches as the boy tears round the room
ignoring the TV which is older than he is
dropping things as quickly as he picks them up.
Betty won't like this mess, Billy's thinking
as the boy tips out drawers onto the worn carpet.
He's wondering how he's going to explain it
when he sees a fistful of medals in the boy's hand.

All of a sudden, he can see
caterpillar tracks across desert sands
can feel the heat of the sun burning into his skin
has the smell of diesel they could never shake.
He remembers, too, how they dealt
with locals they thought were thieving.
Men hung by their wrists, while Tommies
took it in turns to beat brown skin till
it turned red, purple, black.
They never came back.
Billy grabs the brown wrist with his shaking hands
and holds on, as tightly as he can.
There's more than one Desert Rat in this room.

Adil has what he wants, he's looking to get out.
The old man stands between him and the door
clutching his wrist in two frail hands.
Billy's determined, and stronger than he looks.
Adil can't shake the old man off.
Before he knows what he's done

Adil's standing centre stage
knife clenched in clenched fist.
Billy's lying on the floor
and the carpets that haven't changed for fifty years
are tinged with crimson.

## Terra Australis

## road to Chinchilla

The road splits the country wide open
ugly as an axe scar, straight as a spear.
On either side, guards of honour:
telegraph poles with stiff limbed salutes.
The old trails sat peaceably on the surface.
The new trails rattle and thunder and hum.

They've hemmed in the country here
tried to tame it
with barbed wire fences and iron gates
using words like 'mine', 'no entry' and 'private'
words which had no currency here.
Country spills out from under the fences
pokes through barbed wire, refuses to be held.
It's trying to tell you it won't be beaten.
One day, it'll break free, reclaim its own.

# lattice screens and inkdrops

Northeast breezes rustle paperbark leaves, pass through
lattice screens and carved wooden gables. Wraparound
decks, sun-baked and peeling, cradle red gum VJs and
bullnose rooves. Jacaranda blossoms trampled underfoot
spatter pavements and pathways with lilac blue inkdrops.
Heatshimmer rises from vertiginous streets which cut
lung-burning trails to cathedrals of shopping. Gladwrap
dressings, flapping in the wind, bandage stinging thighs
and red raw tattoos. A grey-haired woman stoops and
murmurs Turrbal to a child with lollies on his mind. Radio
presenters discussing taxis colour the airwaves with mock
Indian accents. Traditional owners perform Welcome to
Country for suited City men on a cropped South Bank
lawn. Asian pedestrians on busy city streets are greeted
with a monotone 'Currycurrycurrycurrycurrycurry'.
Licence plate stickers on a dirt-crusted ute proclaim
'100% Aussie' and 'Fuck Off, We're Full'.

## Queensland Kanaka Labour Traffic

*(inspired by descriptions of the Pacific Islander labour trade – referred to by opponents as Queensland Kanaka Labour Traffic.)*

## saltwater boys and Marys

A touch of the tip of the GA's quill –
signed on; *you get 'em plenty kaikai.*

Signed for three years or signed for six
moons but taken for three years.

In the hold others who boarded to barter
– tobacco axe pipe – saw their canoes

shattered by pig iron dropped
from the deck; or were startled from sleep

by fire kindled in their village, fled
into ambush; or were sold for seventy pounds

of tobacco, two or three sovereigns,
Brummagem muskets which, when fired,

would explode. Chained to a ringbolt
or constrained in the hull, saltwater

boys and Marys – from New Guinea,
Ellice, across the Pacific – leaving

for plantation labour. Five pounds a head –
licence to import; twenty pounds a head –

recruiter's fee; six pounds a year wage –
for those who received it. Woken

by dogs dispatched into humpies, half
a loaf and tea brewed from leftovers,

two ounces of beef for the lucky –
skallywag cuts from diseased cattle

usually killed for their skins. Cut cane
from 'can see' to 'can't see'. Sometimes,

Marys gave birth in the fields. When
illness struck doctors were called

not to treat the sick, but to know
what to write on death certificates.

Three years later, those who survived
taken home; or to another island,

any island; or cut loose no job no food
no passage; or headed home

down in the hold, but brought
back to plantations – round trip no-one

bargained for. Immigration Act, no
longer required, rounded up. Last time

in the hold, one-way trip, whether
it was wanted or not.

Men booted and hatted; women in
long linen dresses.

Sixty thousand came, sixteen
hundred allowed to remain.

saltwater boys and Marys

# the returns were all in good health

*(The* Empreza *was a vessel engaged in Queensland Kanaka Labour Traffic in 1893.*
*Found poem.)*


The *Empreza* left Brisbane with one hundred and fifty-three return
    islanders
These returns were then all in good health
Eight days out from Brisbane the *invalids were getting extra food*
A native died from consumption
A kanaka died from *inflammation of the bowels*
His countrymen say he was ill
before he left his plantation on the Herbert River
The returns all left Brisbane in good health

On February 3rd five returns were landed on Futuna
One of the five was a half-caste child suffering from dysentery
The disease soon spread among the natives with terrible fatality
One hundred and thirty-three natives of the island died in three months
The returns all left Brisbane in good health

On February 16th five returns were landed on Erromanga
One was suffering from dysentery in the last stages of the disease
An epidemic was the result in which forty-eight natives died
Next day a child died on board
Two days later a return died from the same cause
and is declared to have been ill before leaving Queensland
The *Empreza*'s passengers left Brisbane in good health

A child died on board in Havannah Harbour from dysentery
Two days later another child died on board and was buried on Epi
On the 6th a female return died
She had been suffering from sores so foul smelling
that she had to be kept by herself
The *Empreza*'s passengers left Brisbane in good health

On March 11th dysentery was general on board
The schooner *Caroline* removed the ninety-two remaining returns
and landed them on thirteen different islands
By this time the *Empreza* was being refitted
On June 4th the recruits and crew are reported all well by the new GA
Inspectors reported the kanaka health to be good from Dan to Beersheba
At least two hundred native lives were sacrificed
and that of a missionary's wife
The returns all left Brisbane in good health

# foundlings

# JACK JOHNSON

## Tommy Burns fight – Rushcutters Bay Sydney, 1908

*before*
*the fight*
*after*

Jack Johnson, the Coloured Heavyweight Champion
of the World, had been prevented from contesting the
Heavyweight Championship of the World for five years by
'the colour bar'. When Tommy Burns became champion in
1906, Johnson chased him around the world for two years
until Burns agreed to fight him in Sydney. Burns received
85% of the purse. Johnson's purse barely covered his costs.

Commentary in print media: Adelle font
Jack Johnson: Orpheus Pro font
Tommy Burns: Mrs Eaves OT font

Hugh 'Huge Deal' D McIntosh was the Australian fight
promoter who organised the Johnson–Burns fight. McIntosh
also refereed the fight, at Johnson's request.

*before*

Please issue
certificate exemption
six months
in favour
Jack Johnson
coloured pugilist


DE BIG COON AM A-COMIN'


Jack Johnson is a colored man but
he is the greatest living exponent of the art of
hit-and-get-away and the outstanding challenger
for the title which Tommy Burns claims
but to which he is not entitled
until he puts Johnson
out of the way

The whole truth is that Burns does
not want to fight me. It is he
and not me who has the
yellow streak

This battle may in the future
be looked back upon as
the first great battle
of an inevitable
race war

There is more in this fight to be
considered than the
pugilistic
title
champion
of the world

'My country, right or wrong,' may be
questioned as a maxim of conduct
but most will confirm
without a moment's doubt
'The White Race Right or Wrong'


Like Micawber I had changed my
place of abode time after time
in expectation of something
turning up but it
never came
to pass


All niggers are alike to me
I'll fight him even though
he
is
a
nigger

It's downright weary work
chasing a man around the world
It makes one real tired

Shame on the money-mad Champion
Shame on the man who upsets
good American precedents
because there are
Dollars Dollars Dollars in it

I'll beat this nigger
or my name isn't
Tommy Burns

Johnson is a big coon
he has a genial face somewhat
babyish of the type of
the little coons
who
may
be
seen
devouring
watermelons

With money in his pocket and
physical triumph over white men in
his heart he displays all the
gross and overbearing
insolence
which makes what we call
the buck nigger
insufferable

In his trousers there were orderly
creases fresh from the tailor's iron. The boots
gleamed not with the vulgar shine of blacking but
with the lustrous gloss of seven dollar patent leather polished
to the point of refraction. Against the ebon darkness of the figure's
Abyssinian neck shone the whiteness of newly-laundered linen
The high collar found fashionable complement in a scarf of
ermine silk adorned with a diamond pin. Afternoon
gloves of pearl-grey suede were carried by a
hand that bore on one of its chocolate-
hued fingers a flashing
gem of rather
more carats
than
one


He is one of the few men of
African blood who in a half-perceiving
way desire to make the white man pay
for the undoubted ill-treatment
of his forebears


The coloured man is accompanied by his wife
a white woman somewhat addicted
to jewellery

There have been
countless women in my life. They
have participated in my triumphs and my
moments of disappointment. They have inspired me and
baulked me; they have been faithful to the utmost
and they have been faithless. Always a
woman has swayed me - sometimes
many have demanded my
attention at the same
moment

Johnson was the great gun of the occasion
he was like an emperor of old

A cloud of attendants surrounds him. The man who
rubs him down doesn't run with him; the runner
doesn't put the gloves on; his sparring partner
does nothing but spar
It resembles the state of things in a big
British household where each
servitor knows his duties

Johnson's training has
consisted largely of champagne
and female society


To my certain knowledge
the black blighter has swallowed
a quart or more of fizz
with his breakfast
every day
for the past month


I used to get up at 6 o'clock
eat an orange and go out on the road
By 9 o'clock I had done all my work
the rest of the time I could spend
driving about in my car
As the people did not
see me doing my
training
they thought
I wasn't doing any

Burns will have the big coloured man's
scalp
dangling from his belt




They are playing hog with me
anyhow and the most
money I can get
out of it is
almost nothing




I was with Burns all the way
He is a white man, and
so am I. Naturally, I
would like to see the
white man
win

I'm going to double-cross all the
schemers in the world and
get the title


All coons are yellow


Citizens who never prayed before
are supplicating Providence to give
the white man a strong
right arm
with
which
to belt
the coon
into oblivion

*the fight*

From the downs of Queensland
shepherds left their charges and miners in
the Golden West threw down their
picks all eager to get
to the fray

They came by street cars
automobiles carriages and on
horseback. Scarcely a tram moved up
William Street that was not laden
to the foot boards. One hour
before the fight was
scheduled to start
every seat
was occupied

Twenty thousand ringside
Twice twenty thousand lingered outside

Not since the days of James J. Corbett has
the prize ring seen so perfect a boxer as Johnson
Long and lithe he is as graceful as
a dancing master and as
true as an arrow
in placing
his
blows


As soon as the crowd spotted him
in his hooded robe the old shouts of
*coon* and *nigger* began


All the hatred of twenty
thousand whites
for
all the
Negroes
in the world

He had not a trouble in the world
When asked what he was going to do after
the fight he said he was going
to the races
It was a
happy prophecy


white beauty
faced
black unloveliness


As the gong sounded Burns
approached Johnson who stood
still smiling with supreme
confidence

Here I am, Tommy. Who
told you I was yellow?

Johnson uppercut Burns so heavily that the
white man was lifted clear off the floor

The world spun crazily a huge
red blur obscured
everything

Even the champagne applied to his
face by his seconds failed
to revive him fully




Poor little Tommy
who told you
you were a fighter?




He played with Burns from the gong
of the opening round to the
finish of the fight

'Hit here, Tommy,' he would say exposing
his unprotected stomach and when
Burns struck Johnson would
neither wince nor
cover up


Come on, Tommy, you can hit
harder than that
can't you?


He would receive the blow with a happy careless
smile directed at the spectators, turn the left side of his
unprotected stomach and say, 'Now there, Tommy.'
Burns would hit as directed. Johnson would
continue to grin and chuckle and
smile his golden smile

Johnson's most pensive and frivolous
taps were like thunderbolts
against Burns' butterfly
flutterings


Principally in the clinches Johnson
rested and smiled and dreamed. This dreaming
expression was fascinating. It was almost
like a trance


As my gaze wandered out into the
surrounding territory I saw a colored
man watching the fight sitting on a fence
My glance returned to him again and
again. He was one of the very few
colored people present

He cuffed and smiled and smiled and
cuffed and in the clinches whirled
his opponent around so as to be
able to assume angelic
expressions
for the
benefit of the
cinematograph machines


Mentally he was fighting harder
than I. Whenever I unlimbered a blow he
too shot one into the air. When I swayed to
avert a blow the fighter on the
fence also swayed in the
same direction


Johnson seemed to ease off in the seventh round
Just as it looked as if Burns could no longer withstand
his attack he allowed the white man to
rest in his arms and recover

He is a funny fellow that Johnson
He stood up before Tommy and would say,
'This is what is known as a left hook,
Tommy,' and he'd let go

Then he'd step back and as Tommy rushed
in would say, 'I will now give you another little
lesson on boxing, Tommy; look out for your
left eye!' Then he'd let go on Burns' eye
He just kidded
Tommy
to
death

I only kidded him in a nice way. But he used
the other sort of language. If I had killed
Burns for the language he used
I would have been
fully justified

Come on and fight, nigger
Fight like a white man

Johnson never ceased smiling when the
uncomplimentary remarks were addressed to him
Nor did he cease smiling as he proceeded to
wallop the naughty boy for his
impertinence. For wallop
him he did

I could have put him away
quicker but I wanted to
punish him. I had
my revenge

In the final round
three heavy right-handed blows
Burns stood in the centre of the ring
swaying to and fro
a touch
would have
knocked him
down


McIntosh shouted
in a voice fit to wake the dead
'Stop, Johnson'


Nobody was sorry to see
Superintendent Mitchell scramble
through the ropes and wave the
giant back to his corner

As McIntosh's voice rebounded
from the walls of that stadium
the mighty concourse
remained silent

Johnson waved his hands
to the crowd
that did not cheer him

*after*

SOUTHERN NEGRO
HEAVYWEIGHT CHAMPION
OF THE WORLD


I had attained my life's ambition
The little Galveston colored
boy had defeated the
world's champion
boxer


Johnson won in every department of
the game and at every stage of
the fight. He represents
a class in himself

My aim was to show Burns after
all his boasting, his talk about the yellow
streak
down
my
spine
that I could
out-box him and
out-slug him


Looking back in memory
I realise I actually
lost that battle
– through hate –
before it started


If I had knocked him
out quickly the public would
have said it was
a
fluke

The fight? There was no
fight. No Armenian massacre could
compare with the hopeless
slaughter
that
took place today

I was positive he would fold up under
punishment. How badly had I underrated
his boxing skill, his tremendous
strength and unquestionable
cunningness

To me it was not a racial triumph
but almost immediately
a hue and cry
went up

Tommy Burns has his price
Thirty thousand dollars
Burns has sold
his pride
the pride of
the Caucasian race


God grant that the defeat of Saturday
may not be the sullen and solemn prophecy
that Australia is to be outclassed and finally vanquished
by these dark-skinned people who everywhere
are beginning to realise their
immense possibilities


For the first and only time in history
a black man held one of the
greatest honours in the
field of sports and
athletics

Already the insolent black's victory causes skin
trouble in Woolloomooloo. An hour after, I heard
a lascar laying down the law
of Queensberry to
two whites
and they listened
humbly. It is a bad day for Australia

Could any Christian nation have extended a
more inhospitable welcome to a
victor of a great contest?

Is the Caucasian played out? Are the races we have been calling
inferior to demand of us that we must draw the color line
in everything if we are to avoid being whipped
individually and collectively?

I must bear your reproaches
because I
beat a white man

**Blessings on the Immigration Restriction Act!**

I never expected sympathy here as my
colour is against me

It is a pity the churchwardens
of Liverpool and Bristol ever went into the
slave trade otherwise Johnson might still
be up a tree in Africa


Jack Johnson, world's heavyweight
boxing champion, arrived in Brisbane
by the RMS *Makura* en
route to
Vancouver


Johnson inquired as to the last resting
place of his prototype the late Peter Jackson
the first coloured champion who
had entitled himself
to be styled
world's best heavyweight boxer

The champion and his wife motored to
Toowong Cemetery. On the quiet picturesque
hillside the living champion spent a few
moments in quiet contemplation




It was an impressive sight. The splendid form
of the living gladiator bending for a moment over
the tomb of he who was Australia's fistic idol
The solemnity of the occasion swept
his now famous smile
from Johnson's
face

# Jim Jeffries fight – 'The Fight of the Century' Reno, 1908

*before*
*mouthfighting*
*Reno*
*fightday*
*aftermath*

Jim Jeffries, Heavyweight Champion of the World, had vacated the title in 1905 rather than fight an African-American boxer for the championship. After Johnson's victory over Tommy Burns, public clamour and a hefty purse lured Jeffries, 'The Great White Hope', back to the ring.

Commentary in print media: Adelle font
Jack Johnson: Orpheus Pro font
Jim Jeffries: Mrs Eaves OT font
*Song playing as Johnson entered the ring: American Scribe*

'Gentleman' Jim Corbett, a past world heavyweight champion, acted as Jeffries' second. He was known for promulgating the triumph of technique over brute force in the ring.

Coloured races outnumber the whites, and have been
kept in subjection by a recognition on their part
of physical and mental inferiority


Draw away the veil of civilisation
you will find the human
race pretty much
equal


Does anyone imagine that
Johnson's success
is without its
political influence?

From the moment he beat Burns he would
not fit in with any well-ordered
scheme of things


Mr Johnson is now lording it over the Caucasian race
All Christendom clamours for a white man to prove by
battering this African upstart into insensibility that
culture morality gentleness intelligence and
all the finer qualities still entitle
the white man to
rule the
black


But one thing remains. Jeffries must emerge from
his alfalfa farm and remove that smile
from Johnson's face. Jeff
it's up to you

All night long I was besieged with telegrams asking me to
re-enter the ring. I answer them now as I have
answered them hundreds of times
I have fought my last fight

The security of white civilisation and white
supremacy depended on the
defeat of Jack
Johnson

I do not care whether Johnson licks the
Japanese army. I will never make
a match with a black man

In science we have advanced
wonderfully but morally precious
little if at all. We should all
cultivate the sense of
fair play

Johnson is a great fighter and a fine fellow
one has only to see him going to understand why Jim
Jeffries sheltered behind that cowardly
protection the colour line

I am the best boxer in the world. I am not only
accepting challenges, I am making them
The man I want is Jim Jeffries

They kept at me. Even in the churches they were
sermonising that I was a skunk
for not defending the white race's honour


When they meet the world will see a battle
before which the gladiator combats of
ancient Rome will pale into
childish insignificance


If I were to whip Johnson I would be hailed
as the greatest champion in
pugilism's history

What Jack Johnson means to do to Jeffries in the
ringed arena will be the ambition of Negroes in
every domain of human endeavour

But to lose to Johnson would
make me a dog

If the black man wins thousands of his ignorant
brothers will misinterpret his victory as justifying claims
to much more than mere physical equality
with their white neighbours

I want to see the championship come
back to the white race
where it belongs

the road is cleared for the long-expected
battle between the black champion and the great
hero the only man to whom we can look to
wrest back the title for the dominant
race. It is not so much a matter
of racial pride as one of
racial existence

I am going into this fight for the
sole purpose of proving
that a white man is
better than a
Negro

*mouthfighting*

That nigger can never lick me



Mistah Johnsing is one of those Africans who look
too black to have the heart of a fighter



All I want is to get him in the ring and
smash his black face

Johnson knows
I hate the ground he walks on
I consider him an accident in the championship class
I propose to give him the worst beating ever given any man
in the ring


It amuses me to hear this talk of Jeffries claiming the
championship. When a mayor leaves office he's
an ex-mayor, isn't he? When a champion
leaves the ring he's an ex-champion


Johnson only has one punch. I have four hundred
every one of them better than his best. I can hit
anywhere from anywhere. Short or long
range from hip or shoulder. I have two
hands. He has one. I can send 'em in
from away off or pound 'em in
with two inches play
Johnson can't

He stands flat-footed as
a washerwoman

yet his footfall is as light and sure as the
step of the swiftest dancer

Lots of people weigh two hundred and eighty pounds –
mostly cutlets. Jeff weighs that in bone and muscle

His wrists are as thick and hairy as a
government mule's leg




You don't catch Jim Jeffries losing
to a colored man




I honestly believe that in pugilism
I am Jeffries' master

It wouldn't be a bad idea for Johnson the black
champion not to forget that he is colored

It is my purpose to demonstrate this
in the most decisive way

Johnson has become reckless
If he ever knew his place
he has forgotten it

The tap of the gong will be
music to me



I dislike Johnson not so much because he is a
negro but because he is one of those fresh negroes
that not alone thinks he is as good
as a white man
but
is
better



He had a penchant for employing
words of wondrous length
but this niggers will do
Johnson was
amusing
in his
pretentiousness

When distressed by criticism of this sort I simply
turn up one or two of my favourite books
Shakespeare's *Titus Andronicus*
Bunyan's *Pilgrims Progress*
or
Milton's *Paradise Lost*
and there I find
plenty consolation
to soothe away any irritation

with the Simian slope of forehead
and the thick African lips
one is taken aback by
the brilliant flow
of Johnson's conversation

The sole reason to account for the
hisses hurled at me was
my racial difference

I have followed the newspaper comments on these two men
for the last twelve months. I have been offended at the
abuse poured over the 'nigger' by the American
papers. That the colored man is the superior
man physically and mentally no
intelligent person can doubt

Why should a man
trying to do what his audience
pays him for be the target of vile
abuse all on account of his
color of skin?

Johnson at least has not to keep people waiting
while he takes the Carlsbad waters
and patches himself up to meet
championship demands

I have found no better way of avoiding race
prejudice than to act with people
of other races as if prejudice
did not exist

God will forgive
everything you do to that
nigger
in this fight

*Reno*

No man who loves the fighting game
has the price and is within striking distance of
Reno should miss the fight

There has never been anything like it in
the history of the ring

An army of unknowns is rapidly gathering
They come tripping forth from Pullmans day-trippers
and smokers; they come tumbling down from
flat-topped box cars or creeping forth
from between the trucks their faces
black with dust

From England and Hawaii, from Australia and
Alaska, in special trains and side-door sleepers. But
globe-trotters or grangers, homebodies hobos gentlemen
or grafters, they are all full-fashioned men with the
love of fighting in their veins. There are
no mollycoddles in Reno


I had an idea Jim was going to do the matinee idol thing
wait until all the other celebrities had made their bow
so we all got off the train ahead of him. Jeffries
jumped off the other side of the train
walked around the rear car and
quietly started for the hotel


For sleeping you take anything you can get: sometimes
a seven-dollar room sometimes a private car
a cot a billiard table a hammock
or a park bench

Johnson quartered like a fussy king

One restaurant with a seating capacity of forty served
three thousand six hundred suppers

Jeffries was as surly and ugly as a caged bear

If a hand was not dipped into your pocket
it was almost a sign of disrespect


In a single day one hundred and fifty thousand words
went out from here over the wires


Johnson is as tall as Jeffries but fully thirty
pounds lighter. There is something of the grace and power
of the panther in the long easy swing of his walk

Once in his private quarters the negro ordered
one of his assistants to load the phonograph
For an hour the hotel was filled with
operatic music – Caruso Sembrich
Nordics. Not once did a
ragtime piece appear

Jeffries is the embodiment of all that is powerful and brutish
in the white man

To all appearances the black man
is as happy and carefree as a
plantation darky
in Watermelon time

I saw that which I never expected to see; a man who has come back. I believe Jeffries to be the most rugged dangerous fighter the world has ever seen

Boxed nine rounds yesterday – Faster
than ever – Can't get the Black to work
hard enough – Had his auto out – Not
training – Corbett'll do it for him –
Too old – Good as ever – Bet you

Johnson drove along the deserted boulevard taking
turns with a swoop that threatened to turn the car
turtle. All the time he was watching out the
corner of his eye the frightened
passengers who hung on
like
leeches
'You ain't afraid, are you?'

The man is a puzzle. Physically
the greatest athlete the colored race has
produced, mentally as keen as a razor in a sort
of undeveloped way but he fiddles away on his bull
fiddle, swaps jokes with ready wit, shoots craps, listens
dreamily to classical love songs on the phonograph
and is going to fight Jim Jeffries for the
world's championship one week
from tomorrow

This Colossus of a white man a sort of grizzly bear
bored by people and noise much preferring to
bury himself in the mountains and fish

Yet you had but to look at that vast body those legs
like trees the long projecting jaw deep-set
scowling eyes and cruel mouth to know
here was an animal
who would give battle whom
cleverness could not ruffle
nor blows dismay

The white man has thirty centuries of tradition behind him
all the supreme efforts the inventions and conquests
Bunker Hill and Thermopylae and
Hastings and Agincourt

The Negro had nothing but the jungle

Our memories are handed down from father to son. Whites don't think
so but we blacks are also proud of our ancestors. During
long days and still longer nights though we knew
neither schools nor books we still transmitted
memories of past centuries

The Negro would be licked the moment the
white man looked him in the eye

He didn't have the dogged courage and intellectual
initiative which is the white man's inheritance

I can lick Jim Jeffries
Jeffries never licked a young man

Thousands of negroes have nailed your
name to their masthead. Nobody
has so much to win or lose
as you represent

On the arid plains of the Sage Brush State
the white man and the negro will settle
the mooted question of supremacy

BET YOUR LAST COPPER ON ME

*fightday*

It was a beautiful day. The weather
excepting for the intense heat was superb
The atmosphere was clear as crystal
One could see for miles

A black streak of humanity stretched from the centre
of town over the single broad road that passes the arena. It was a
stream constantly augmented from side streets pulsing
shifting with cross currents wavering in the channel

You must imagine a bright green little oasis set
in a dish of bare enclosing mountains – brown mountains
with patches of yellow and olive-green and exquisite
veils of mauve and amethyst, and at their tops,
blazing white in the clear air, patches
of austere snow
In the centre of all this a
great
pine
bear pit
had been raised

More than twenty thousand people had gathered
As I scanned that sea of white faces, I felt
the auspiciousness of the occasion




Every manner of man was in it. A miner
from Rhyolite with trousers tucked inside his half-boots, a
Chinaman padding the dust with his felt shoes, a clubman from
Frisco with a jewelled pin in his coat, a flashy race-tout
from New Orleans, overdressed Japanese who carried
insolence in their eyes, plain dips and stickup men
mine owners stock brokers touts blacklegs
politicians bank presidents
and second-story men




There were few men of my own race amongst the spectators.
I was well aware that most of that great audience was
hostile to me. These things did not disturb or
worry me. I was perfectly at ease

They hadn't come to see a fight
they had come to witness an execution

Mrs Johnson was the prettiest woman in the place. Apparently
a white woman and becomingly gowned

I have the right to choose
whom my mate shall be without
the dictation of any man
I am not a slave

The first blood cry of the thousands
echoed
as the men climbed into the ring


The black man was the first to strip
when he stepped forth for the lenses to
register his image he was a thing
of surpassing beauty

from the
anatomist's
point of view


I have never seen a human being more calculated to
strike terror into an opponent's heart as this Colossus as he
came through the ropes stamped like a bull pawing the ground
and glared at the black man across the ring

No facile emotion played on that face
no whims of the moment no flutterings of a
light-hearted temperament. Dark and sombre and
ominous was that face with eyes that
smouldered and looked savage

So friendly was that smile of Johnson
so irresistibly catching that Jeff
despite himself
smiled back

I don't suppose that one man in a hundred
would have given two cents
for the negro's chances

*All coons look alike to me*

Hats waved flags fluttered feeling
ran high – Patriotism was riot

Let's hope he kills the coon

the contest
white man's hope
the black peril

First blood to Jeff. Men who had never seen
each other before slapped each other on the back
and said 'Jeff's getting in his work'
or 'it'll soon be over'

Mr Jim Corbett, Jeffries' second, following the quaint
sportsmanship of the ring had gone across to the negro
between rounds to fix him with a sneering eye
and wittily taunt and terrify him

Nor did many suspect – so strong was the Jeffries
tradition the contagion of the atmosphere and that crouching
scowling gladiator – that the negro's finish was
anything but a matter of time

He'll kill you, Jack
That's what they all say

They had all seen the white man send in time and
time again with tremendous force that piston-rod punch
into his opponent's side. Each time the crowd
gave a subdued exultant grunt

He'll straighten you up, nigger


When Johnson merely smiled his faraway
smile people supposed he must be shamming and
when those uppercuts of his shot up like
lightning they thought it was
pretty but didn't hurt


Jeffries tried to wear Johnson down
by his weight in the clinches
All right, Jim. I'll
love you if you want me to

Johnson's left shot across to the white man's
right eye in the sixth round and closed it

The cynicism of the white man's glare suddenly
changed. He was fighting after that not to finish
off his opponent but to save himself

My eyes could detect openings or danger. But my muscles
wouldn't respond as quickly to the dictates of
the brain. They were slow, slow, slow

Come on, now, Mr Jeff. *Do* something
This is for the championship

The big man bleeding beaten but glaring
out of his one good eye bored steadily in as
the bull charges the matador
towards the end

All at once his tree-like legs caved in and the great
hairy bulk which had never been knocked
down before nor beaten sank
close to the ropes

A great silence fell a guttural
gust of pity came
from twelve thousand chests

The crowd didn't cheer. It rose and stood and
stared as if the solid ground beneath it
were turning to a mirage

Mister Jack Arthur Johnson with only a slightly cut
lip rode back to his camp in his automobile

it is to be doubted if the old Jeff could have
put away this amazing negro this black
man with the unfailing smile
this king of
fighters
and
monologists

I could never have whipped Jack Johnson
at my best. I couldn't have reached him
in a thousand years

I could have fought for two hours longer

Anyone who happened to see the face
of Jim Jeffries as he climbed into the ring
felt the focussed mind and heard the taunts
and the jeers of the hostile crowd knows
it took more than boxing skill
for that black man
to go out
and meet his fate

*aftermath*

I knew he would do it
There were eighty million people against
him but he beat them all. It certainly is grand to be
the mother of a real hero. If his father
had only lived to see it

The gritty old woman stood and sang
so long that hoarseness robbed her of her voice so
she just stood and cried

The Negroes were jubilant. Everybody wanted to buy
someone else a dinner a glass of beer or a shot of whiskey. Older
people laughed and cried, and children danced. Grandma Thompson raised
her quivering voice in song. We all joined in. We were
now a race of champions

Rioting broke out like prickly heat
all over the country

The black man were he of white skin doubtless would be the
most popular champion we ever had. He has all the manners
to make him such. No matter the request Johnson is
willing to go out of his way to grant it. He is
sunny Jack for sure

When whites in Wheeling, West Virginia
came upon a Negro driving a handsome automobile
they dragged him out from behind the steering wheel
and hanged him

Johnson promised an old-timer who taught Johnson how to
fight on the docks that if he ever got to be champion he would
buy the old man two suits and a red necktie. Sure enough he
kept his promise and sent word to order two
suits of clothes and not to be
stingy with the price


In the 'black and tan' and 'San Juan hill' negro sections mobs
set fire to a negro tenement house and tried to keep
the occupants in by blocking the exits


Just because my black fists happened to be
too many for a pair of white fists

A word to the Black Man
Do not point your nose too high. Do not swell
your chest too much. Do not be puffed up. Let not your ambition be
inordinate. Remember you have done nothing at all. You are just the same
member of society you were last week. You are on no higher plane deserve
no new consideration and will get none. No man will think higher
of you because your complexion is the same
as that of the victor at Reno

It was a good deal better for Johnson to win and a few Negroes
be killed in body for it than for Johnson to have lost and
Negroes to have been killed in spirit by
the preachments of inferiority

I only hope the colored people of the world will not be
like the French. History tells us when Napoleon was winning
the French were with him but when he lost, the people
turned against him. When Jack Johnson meets
defeat, I want the colored people
to love me the same as when I
was the champion

The reason Jack Johnson was so beset by his own country
a country ironically which had recently reaffirmed that
all men were created equal
was because
of his
Unforgivable Blackness

# BORIS JOHNSON

*(Found poems derived from Boris Johnson's writings)*

## *piccaninnies*


>
> the Queen has come to love the Commonwealth
> because it supplies her with regular cheering crowds of
>
> flag-waving piccaninnies

Blair      is similarly seduced
     the tribal warriors will all break out    in Watermelon smiles

to see the big white chief touch down
     in his big white British taxpayer-funded bird

# pearl of Africa

The continent may be a blot but it is not a blot
upon our conscience

The problem is not that we were once in charge
but that we are not in charge
any more

Consider Uganda
pearl of Africa

If left to their own devices    the natives would rely on nothing
but the instant carbohydrate gratification          of the plantain

The best fate for Africa would be    if the old colonial powers
or their citizens

scrambled once again in her direction

on the understanding that this time

they will not be asked to feel guilty

## part-Kenyan

when Barack Obama entered the Oval Office
something vanished from that room


a bust of Winston Churchill


it was a symbol
of the          part-Kenyan President's
ancestral dislike of the British empire


perhaps Churchill was      less important
his ideas     out of date


if that's why Churchill was banished


they could not have been more wrong

CHURCHILL

**in his own words**

I hate people with
slit eyes and pig-tails. I don't
like the look of them or the smell of them.

I hate Indians. They are a beastly people with a
beastly religion.

The Arabs were barbaric hordes who ate
little but camel dung.

I do not admit     that a great wrong has been done to the Red
Indians of America, or the black people of Australia
by the fact that             a higher-grade race
has come in and taken their place.

I do not understand this squeamishness     about the use of gas.

I am strongly in favour of using poisoned gas
against uncivilised tribes.

Why be apologetic about Anglo-Saxon
superiority? We are superior.

Keep          England          White

The Aryan stock is bound
to triumph.

OBAMA

**in the words of others**


                                        Can you just
                            show us
                                        the birth certificate?

Barack Obama's mother
        was living
                                        there is something
                                                on that
                    in Kenya            birth certificate

with his Arab-
African father                          maybe
   late in her pregnancy                religion
                                        maybe
She was not allowed                     it says he's a
    to travel     so Barack Obama was   Muslim
         born there

                                            In the mind
    Here is a man who          of the average American
   spent the first                  there is    no doubt
seventeen years                     he is a Muslim
of his life off
   the American mainland     the anti-colonial ideology of Barack
      Hawaii              Obama Sr is  espoused by his son the
            Indonesia     President of
                 Pakistan                   the United States


    The US is being ruled
              according to          Ayatollah Obama
      the dreams of a Luo tribesman
         of the 1950s

epilogue

## my son

The kids on the street fight with you
as if you were their brother. You play
line-tiggy Minecraft hide-and-seek
share icy poles banana bread sticky bowls of chips.
The red-haired Celt two years older than you
tells us not to worry when you start school.
She will look after you and next year when
her brother starts school you will look after him.
The woman three houses up takes you on trips
with her children buys your favourite *won ton meen*
spoils you as she spoils her own son and daughter.
Perhaps that is simply long-term planning.
Her daughter and you, born three weeks apart,
decided at school that you would marry
and move to the UK so you could play in the snow.

The Ashes is on in the background. We are playing
Monopoly. Usman Khawaja comes on the screen.
Pakistan-born, the first Asian to play for Australia
they say he would have played more
if he hadn't been so lazy
they say he would have played more
if he looked as if he cared
they say he would have played more
if his name were Thomson or Hughes

*I like him. He has dark skin, like me.*

You drop your bomb and carry on
buying up the Old Kent Road.
Your mother and I stare
*where did that otherness come from*
and I am falling
*who said what to you and when*
through the hoop pine floorboards of our Queenslander
*how did we not know*
through the cloying red clay underneath
*what have you seen and not seen*
dirt in my nose and mouth and eyes
*how is this happening here*
I can't breathe for thinking
*how is this happening so far from there*
      from the National Front and Union Jacks
      from dogshit through letterboxes
      from milk bottles thrown at schoolchildren
      from milk bottles thrown *by* schoolchildren
      from the chants
*SKINHEAD SKINHEAD SKINHEAD*
from twenty or thirty or more
men with bovver boots and Nazi salutes
that boom across the station concourse
fill that vast space
fill my ears until I can hear nothing else
not the train announcement with its comforting
*West Dulwich Sydenham Hill Penge*
not the unconcerned chatter of the pony-tailed brunette next to me
the sound itself is an assault I try to close out

knowing in that congestion of late commuters and early revellers
        I am alone
knowing eye contact is a mistake I will make only once
knowing amongst all these people I am the one they will come for

Clawing my way up through the clay I ask
        *Must I fight this fight again?*
        *From the day I sat in my first class*
        *five years old and freshly arrived*
        *this fight will not leave me alone*

        you sit in a classroom with
        Indigenous art on the walls
        your kindy mates correct the cricket coach
        on his pronunciation of your name
        no-one on the street thinks twice when we speak
        Sinhala in our home or theirs
        yet a sense of separateness
        has seeped into you

From the darkness the answer comes
        *yes*
        *now*
        *more than ever*

# Notes

*blackbirds don't mate with starlings* arose from the global response to the terrible murder of George Floyd. Building on the backlash from people of all races whose protests indicated they refused to accept these injustices any longer, this collection uses stories disseminated in time and place to demonstrate how present-day injustices have taken root in our societies, and to emphasise the need to counter those injustices wherever and whenever they arise.

**'triptych – past present future'**
Cannon-balling was a method of execution used by the British in India. The Russian war painter Vasily Vereshchagin depicted the execution of Namdharis, a peaceful Sikh sect, by cannon-balling in his painting *Suppression of the Indian Revolt by the English*.

**'how dare they'**
The shooting of Cherry Groce in her home by the Metropolitan Police sparked the 1985 Brixton race riots.

Cynthia Jarrett died from a heart attack during a Metropolitan Police raid on her home. Her death led to the Broadwater Farm race riot, a week later.

Christopher Alder died in police custody in 1998. Five police officers were acquitted of manslaughter in 2002. There is CCTV footage from Queens Garden Police Station, Kingston upon Hull, of four officers standing over his unconscious body and making monkey noises.

**'desert rat'**
Inspired by home visits to the Downham Estate in Lewisham, and by North African refugees in Peckham, south-east London.

**'saltwater boys and Marys'**
Inspired by descriptions of the Pacific Islander labour trade by W Gray and in *Me No Go Mally Bulla: Recruiting and blackbirding in the Queensland labour trade 1863–1906* by Wal Bird.

A 'GA' is a government agent.

In contemporaneous accounts it is recorded that Pacific Islanders, when conversing with recruiters and government agents, referred to themselves as 'saltwater boys' and 'Marys'.

**'the returns were all in good health'**
A found poem using quotations from *The Kanaka or How Queensland Planters Get and Treat Their* — by W Gray, published in 1895.

**'Jack Johnson', 'Boris Johnson', 'Churchill' and 'Obama'**
Found poems derived from first-person quotations, contemporaneous accounts, newspaper articles, and transcripts of radio and television broadcasts.

Particularly important to telling the Jack Johnson story are Jack Johnson's autobiographies *In the Ring and Out* and *Ma Vie et Mes Combats* (serialised in *La Vie au Grand Air*), as well as his Fort Leavenworth papers.

Also invaluable were: *Unforgivable Blackness: The rise and fall of Jack Johnson* by Geoffrey C Ward; *Papa Jack: Jack Johnson and the era of white hopes* by Randy Roberts; *Bad Nigger! The national impact of Jack Johnson* by Al-Tony Gilmore; 'The Australian Reaction to Jack Johnson, American Pugilist, 1907–09' by Richard Broome; *The Fight of the Century: Jack Johnson, Joe Louis and the struggle for racial equality* by Thomas R Hietala; *Black Manhattan* by James Weldon Johnson; *A Beautiful Pageant: African American theatre drama and performance in the Harlem Renaissance 1910–1927* by David Krasner; 'The Negro's Smile, Story of a Big Fight' by Jack London; 'In Reno Riotous' by Harris Merton Lyon; 'The Fight in the Desert' by Arthur Ruhl; and *Boxing Day: The fight that changed the world* by Jeff Wells.

For full details of source material and quotations, go to uqp.com/books/blackbirds-dont-mate-with-starlings

# Acknowledgements

I would like to thank the editors of *Cordite Review* and *Peril* magazine, in which some of these poems appeared in earlier forms. Thanks in particular to Eleanor Jackson, an early and consistent supporter.

I would like to thank Queensland Poetry and the Arts Queensland Thomas Shapcott Poetry Prize for this opportunity. I am humbled by the care and attention the UQP team has taken over the collection. My thanks to all at UQP, especially Aviva Tuffield, my publisher, and Margot Lloyd.

I owe Felicity Plunkett, my editor, a great debt for her eye and her ear and her perspicacity. The poem 'my son' owes its existence to her vision. Thank you.

I cannot thank by name all the people who have walked this writerly journey with me over the past decade and more. I am truly grateful for all the help I have had along the way. Mention must go to Tim Clarke, Afdhel Aziz (and his injunction to stop pootling) and Peter Basile.

A big London hug to Shane Solanki – The Last Mango in Paris – who first shoved me on stage with a mic in my hand and made me believe I might be on to something.

Emily Moorefield's tutelage, at a critical time in my poetry journey, left a deep imprint on my writing. Thanks and warm wishes from afar.

My thanks to my friends in poetry who have helped shape these poems and shape me as a poet: amongst others, Trudie Murrell, Lee-Anne Davie, Tamara Lazaroff, Jonathan Hadwen, Andrew 'Prawns' Phillips, Chloë Callistemon, and Vanessa Page; and to Mirandi Riwoe for her ebullient encouragement.

Thanks to the aunties, uncles, cousins and friends, in Sri Lanka and elsewhere, who are my hinterland.

Special thanks to my cousin Ranil, for his assistance with pretty much everything.

My love and gratitude to Ammi, Thaththi and Malli, for everything you have done; to Lana and her reservoirs of patience; and to Nisara, a constant inspiration.